I0172243

This Book Belongs To

_____
_____

ISBN: 978-0615871127

Library of Congress Control Number: 2013915329

Copyright: TXu-1-852-223

Aunt L Books and Merchandise is available at
www.AuntLBooks.com

Melvin, The Melancholy Mouse

by Aunt L.

illustrations by
Maksym Stasiuk

Dedicated to my grandson, Emerson, my little angel, who is never melancholy. Special thanks to my husband who believes in my dreams.

Melvin is a garden mouse. A little brown garden mouse. He lives in Aunt L's vegetable garden on the side of her house. Melvin is always sad. No one calls him Melvin. All the creatures in the garden call him Melancholy.

One sunny day, Melvin came out of his home under a pile of pine needles. He looked around the garden and noticed everyone was happy. They were happy everyday. He wanted to be happy too. He was going to find out how to be happy.

Melvin walked over to a long stemmed daisy with two beautiful orange dragonflies resting on the bright yellow flower. Melvin asked, "Why are you two orange dragonflies always happy?" The dragonflies answered, "Hi Melancholy, when we fly, our transparent wings glow and twinkle. That is what makes us happy."

"Um," thought Melvin, "maybe I need twinkle wings to make me happy." He pulled some dead basil leaves off a plant. The leaves were almost see through. Melvin tied the leaves around his tiny front feet. Melvin climbed atop a small rock glistening in the sun. The leaves twinkled. But it did not make Melvin happy.

Melvin saw a couple of his toad friends sitting under a mossy covered log in the corner of the garden. He asked them, "Why are you two toads always happy?" The toads looked at Melvin and answered "Melancholy, we get to fill our bellies by eating yummy slugs in the garden. That is what makes us happy.

"Well," thought Melvin, "I have never eaten a slug, maybe that will make me happy." He stuck his little pink nose under the log and pulled out a slimy slug. He licked the slug. "Yuck," cried Melvin, "slugs do not taste good." It did not make Melvin happy.

Melvin wandered to the garden gate where he met a pair of moles popping up from the ground to get some fresh air. He asked them, "Why are you two moles always happy?" The moles looked at Melvin and answered, "We love smelling the warm moist dirt when we tunnel under the garden. That is what makes us happy, Melancholy."

"Interesting," thought Melvin. He had never made a tunnel to smell dirt. Melvin put his front paws together. He began to dig a tunnel in the garden. Melvin stuck his nose and face deep into the tunnel. He took a long sniff. "Oh my," said Melvin, "I have dirt stuck in my nose. This does not make me happy."

A pair of white bunnies munching on leafy parsley were watching Melvin dig the tunnel. "Hey Melancholy, what are you doing?" asked the bunnies. Melvin answered, "I am trying to find out what makes everyone happy". The bunnies wiggled their pink noses, smiled, and said, "That's simple. Hopping. Everyone knows that hopping makes you happy."

Melvin had never hopped. He thought, "Maybe that was why he wasn't happy." Melvin tucked his front legs under his chin. He hopped on his back legs. He fell forward bumping his little nose on the ground. Hopping did not make him happy.

No one in the garden could help him. Melvin was very unhappy.

Melvin headed home. When he passed the garden gate he saw a small furry head sneaking underneath. Melvin stopped. It was a grey field mouse creeping into Aunt L's garden. Melvin was surprised. He had never seen another mouse. The field mouse said, "Hello, my name is Sam. This looks like a nice place to live. Would you show me around the garden?"

Melvin showed Sam around the garden. They shared a bush bean growing against the garden wall for lunch. When they finished eating, Melvin showed Sam more of the garden. They met the dragonflies. They met the toads. They met the moles. They met the bunnies. They laughed, they played and they shared stories until it was night.

Melvin asked Sam, "Would you care to stay with me at my house under the soft pine needles? I have never had anyone to share with, I like sharing with you."

Sam quickly answered, "This is a nice garden. It would be wonderful to share your pine needle home.

Sam and Melvin strolled to the corner of Aunt L's garden. They shared a dried jujube for dinner. After dining, they scurried to bed under the big pile of pine needles.

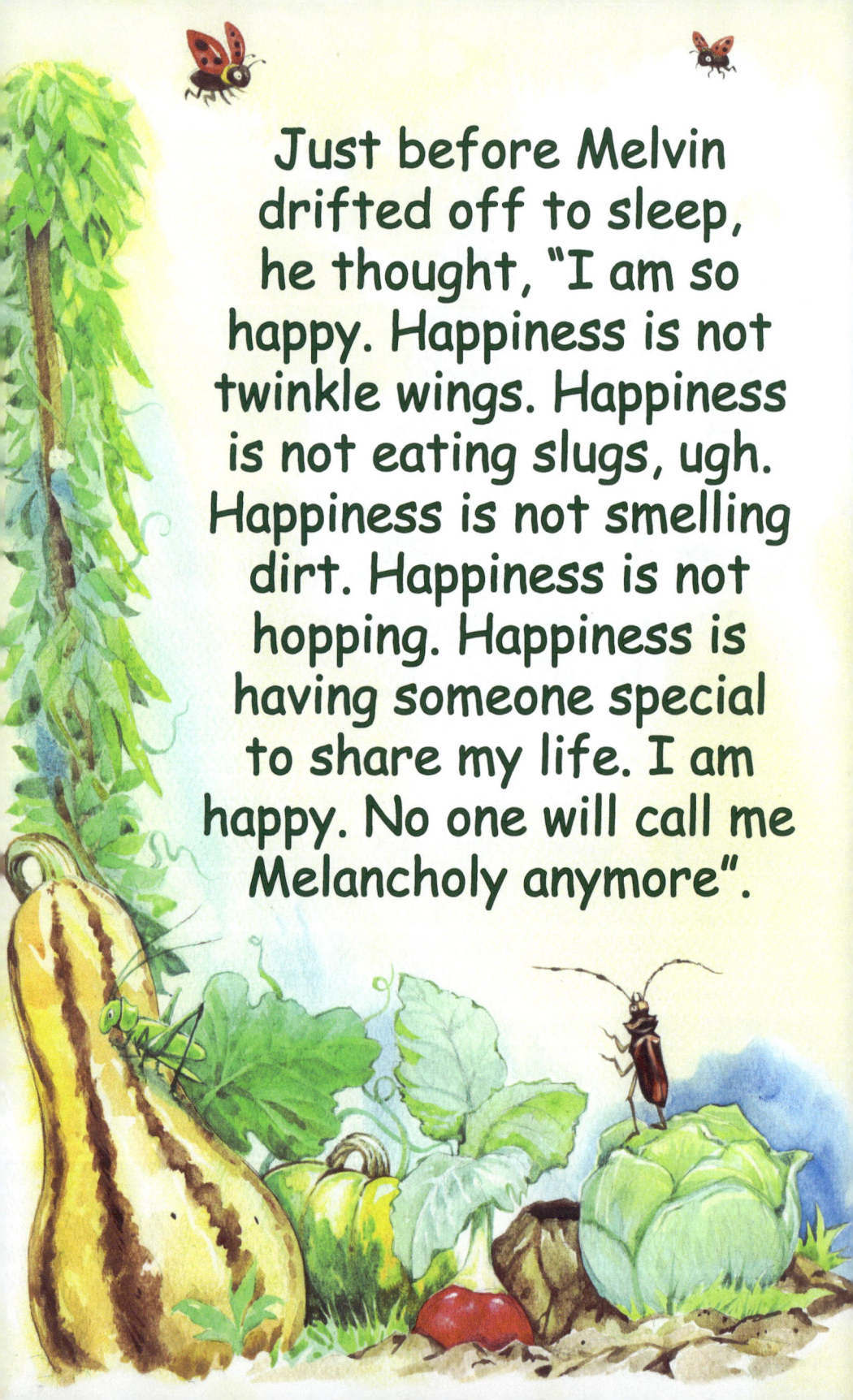

Just before Melvin drifted off to sleep, he thought, "I am so happy. Happiness is not twinkle wings. Happiness is not eating slugs, ugh. Happiness is not smelling dirt. Happiness is not hopping. Happiness is having someone special to share my life. I am happy. No one will call me Melancholy anymore".

www.ingramcontent.com/pod-product-compliance
Lightning Source LLC
Chambersburg PA
CBHW041808040426
42449CB00001B/16